# MY BIG BOOK OF WORDS and PICTURES

*Written by Colin Clark*

*Illustrated by Vivienne Bray*
*and Judy Hensman*

## Brown Watson
ENGLAND

# Aa

### acrobat
An **acrobat** does jumping and balancing tricks.

### actor
An **actor** pretends to be another person in a film or a play.
The children are **acting**.

### address
The **address** on a letter says where you live.
You live at your **address**.

## aircraft

An **aircraft** is a machine that flies in the sky.

## airport

You can see lots of **aircraft** landing and taking off at an **airport**.

## alphabet

All the words that we speak or write are made up of the letters of the **alphabet**.

## ambulance

An **ambulance** takes sick people to hospital.

## animal

Any living thing that can move about and feel is called an **animal**.
Here are some pictures of **animals**.

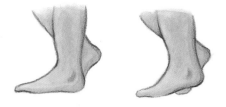

### ankle
The **ankle** is the part of our body that joins the leg to the foot.

### apple
An **apple** is a fruit.
**Apples** are good to eat, and they are good for us.

### apron
When someone is cooking, they wear an **apron** to keep their clothes clean.

### arm
Your **arm** is between your shoulder and your hand.
We have two **arms**.

### arrow
An **arrow** is fired through the air from a bow.
The head of an **arrow** is very sharp.

### artist

The person painting the picture is called an **artist**.

### astronaut

An **astronaut** is someone who travels out into space. Some **astronauts** have been to the Moon.

### axe

An **axe** is a sharp tool for cutting wood.
Jack cut down the beanstalk with an **axe**.

# B b

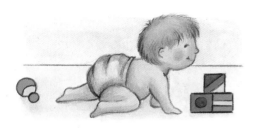

## baby
A **baby** is a very young child.
**Babies** crawl about on their hands and knees.

## back
The children are standing **back** to **back**. The **backs** of their bodies are touching.

## badge
The boy has a **badge** on his jumper.

## bag
You can carry lots of things in a **bag**.

7

## ball

Some games are played with a **ball**. **Balls** can be different shapes and sizes.

## balloon

We blow a **balloon** full of air. We have **balloons** at parties.

## banana

A **banana** is a fruit. We peel off the yellow skin before we eat a **banana**.

## band

A **band** is a group of people who make music together. This **band** is playing loudly.

### barn

Farmers keep their cows
and hay in a **barn**.

### basket

The man has a large **basket**
of flowers.

### bat

This flying animal is a **bat**.

In some games, we hit a ball
with a **bat**.

## bath

We wash ourselves all over in the **bath**.

## beach

The sandy part beside the sea is called the **beach**.

## bear

A **bear** is a large, furry, wild animal.

## bed
We lie down in a **bed** when we want to sleep.

## bee
A **bee** is a buzzing insect. **Bees** live in a hive and make honey.

## bell
A **bell** rings when it is time to go to school.

## berry
A **berry** is a juicy fruit with little seeds in it.

## bicycle
We can ride a **bicycle**. A **bicycle** has two wheels.

## bird

A **bird** is an animal with wings and feathers. Most **birds** can fly. Here are some **birds**.

## black

**Black** is a very dark colour. The hat is **black**.

## blue

**Blue** is a colour. The sky is **blue** and so are the balloons.

## boat

You travel over water in a **boat**.
The children are in a rowing **boat**.

## book

This girl is reading a **book**.
This dictionary is a **book**.

## boot

A **boot** covers part of the leg as well as the foot. When it rains, we wear rubber **boots**.

## bottle

A **bottle** holds something wet, like water, or milk, or lemonade, or tomato sauce.

## bow

We use a **bow** for shooting arrows.

## boy

A male child is a **boy**.

## bridge

We use a **bridge** to cross over something, like a road, a railway, or a river.

## brown

**Brown** is a colour.
The coat is **brown**.
So is the Teddy bear.

## brush

We use a **brush** for painting or cleaning.
We **brush** our hair.

## bulldozer

A **bulldozer** can move piles of earth or rubble.

## bus

A **bus** can carry people along the road. The children are in the school **bus**.

## butterfly

A **butterfly** is an insect with four large wings. Some **butterfies** are very colourful.

# Cc

**cage**
Sometimes we keep pet birds or mice in a **cage**.

**cake**
A **cake** is sweet and baked in the oven. On our birthday, we have a birthday **cake**.

**camel**
A **camel** is an animal with one or two humps on its back. **Camels** live in the desert.

**candle**
A **candle** gives us light.

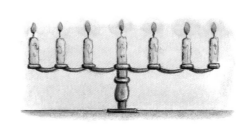

## car

We travel by **car** along the road.

## castle

A **castle** is a large, old building with thick stone walls and towers.

## cat

A **cat** is a furry animal. We keep **cats** as pets.

## caterpillar

A **caterpillar** is long and soft, with lots of legs. A **caterpillar** changes into a moth or a butterfly.

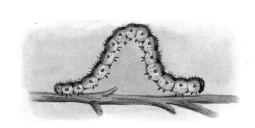

## cherry

A **cherry** is a small, round, tasty fruit. **Cherries** are sweet and good to eat.

## chicken

A **chicken** is a bird. These baby **chickens** are called chicks.

## chimney

The smoke from the fire goes up the **chimney**.

## Christmas

December 25th is **Christmas**, the birthday of Jesus. We give presents at **Christmas**.

## clock
A **clock** shows us the time.

## clothes
All the things we wear are
called **clothes**.

## cot
A baby sleeps in a little bed
called a **cot**.

## cow
A **cow** is an animal that
gives us milk.

## crab

A **crab** lives in the sea.
**Crabs** can nip you
with their claws.

## crane

A **crane** is a machine which
lifts large, heavy things.

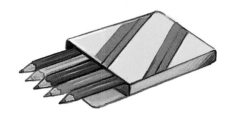

## crayon

We can use a **crayon** to
colour a drawing.

## cup

We drink something out of
a **cup**.

# D d

### dancer

A **dancer** moves about in time to music.

### deer

**Deer** are shy, wild animals.

### dentist

A **dentist** is someone who helps us to keep our teeth shining and healthy.

## desk

We can sit at a **desk** when we want to read or write.

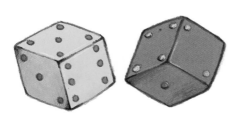

## dice

We use a dice to play some games. A dice has six sides.

## dinosaur

A **dinosaur** is an animal that lived a long, long time ago. Some **dinosaurs** were big and fierce.

**doctor**

When we are sick, a **doctor** will take care of us.

**dog**

A **dog** is a friend.
Some **dogs** are big, and
some are small.

**doll**

A **doll** is a toy that looks like
a person. We can play with
a **doll**.

**donkey**

A **donkey** is an animal
with long ears.
**Donkeys** say: 'Hee-Haw'.

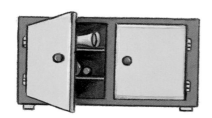

**door**

A room or a cupboard has a
**door**. We can open and
close a **door**.

## dragon

In fairy tales, a **dragon** is a fire-breathing animal with wings.

## dress

A girl or a woman will wear a **dress**.

## drum

We can make music with a **drum** by hitting it with **drum**sticks.

## duck

A **duck** says: 'Quack, quack'. **Ducks** are birds that can swim and fly.

# Ee

**eagle**
An **eagle** is a big bird with strong claws. **Eagles** make their nests in high places.

**ear**
On each side of our head, we have an **ear**.
We hear with our **ears**.

**eggs**
Birds and some other animals lay **eggs**.
We can eat some **eggs**.

**elbow**
Our arms bend in the middle at the **elbow**.

## elephant

An **elephant** is a large, grey animal with big ears, and a very long nose, called a trunk.

## empty

The box is **empty**.
There is nothing in the box.

## end

The **end** is the last of something. Each dog has an **end** of the rope.

## envelope

When we have written a letter, we put it into an **envelope** before we post it.

| n | o | p | q | r | s | t | u | v | w | x | y | z |
|---|---|---|---|---|---|---|---|---|---|---|---|---|
| N | O | P | Q | R | S | T | U | V | W | X | Y | Z |

## Eskimo

An **Eskimo** lives in a very cold part of the world. **Eskimos** have to wear warm, furry clothes.

## exercises

The children are doing **exercises**. **Exercises** are special movements to keep our bodies fit.

## eye

The **eye** is the part of our body through which we see. We have two **eyes**.

# Ff

**face**

The **face** is on the front of the head.

**fair**

We can have lots of fun at a **fair**.

**farm**

On a **farm**, food is grown and **farm** animals are kept.

## feather
A **feather** is very light.
**Feathers** grow on birds.

## fence
You put a **fence** of wood
or wire round your garden.

## finger
A **finger** is a part of the
hand. On each hand, we
have four **fingers** and a
thumb.

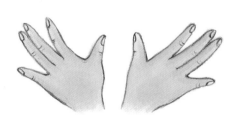

## fire
When something is burning,
there is a **fire**. A **fire** is very
hot.

## fish
A **fish** is an animal that
lives in water.

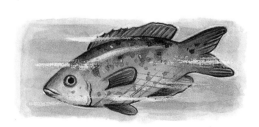

## flag

A **flag** is a coloured piece of cloth or paper. This is the pirates' **flag**.

## flowers

**Flowers** are pretty to look at and they smell nice.
A **flower** is the part of a plant with seeds in it.

## food

**Food** is what we eat. Everything needs **food** to stay alive.

## foot

At the end of each leg, we have a **foot**. We stand on our **feet**.

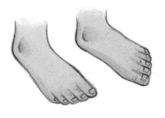

## forest

There are lots of trees in a **forest**.

## fountain

A **fountain** shoots water up into the air.

## fox

A **fox** is a kind of wild dog, with a bushy tail.

## frog

A **frog** is a small animal that lives near water. **Frogs** croak and jump, and they have webbed feet.

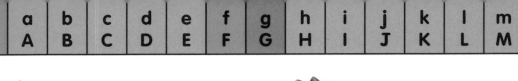

## fruit

Some plants have **fruit**. We eat **fruit**, like oranges, bananas, strawberries and pineapples.

## full

When you cannot get any more into something, it is **full**.

## funny

The clown makes the children laugh. They think the clown is **funny**.

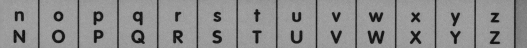

| n | o | p | q | r | s | t | u | v | w | x | y | z |
|---|---|---|---|---|---|---|---|---|---|---|---|---|
| N | O | P | Q | R | S | T | U | V | W | X | Y | Z |

# G g

## garage
The car is in the **garage**.

## garden
A **garden** is some land on which we grow grass and flowers. We can play in the **garden**.

## gate
A **gate** is like a door in a fence. We open the **gate** to get into the garden.

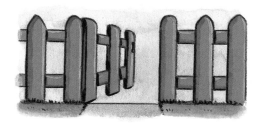

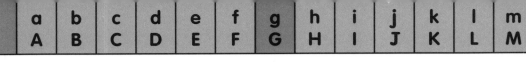

## giant
A **giant** is a very big person in a fairy-tale.

## giraffe
A **giraffe** is a wild animal with long legs and a very long neck.

## girl
A female child is a **girl**.

## gloves
We wear **gloves** to keep our hands warm.

## goat
A **goat** is like a large sheep with horns and a beard.

## goldfish
We keep **goldfish** as pets in a tank, or in a pond in the garden.

## grass
**Grass** is green, and grows almost everywhere. We have to cut the **grass** in the garden.

## green
**Green** is a colour. The jumper is **green**. So is the scarf.

## grey
**Grey** is a colour. Clouds are **grey** when it is raining.

# Hh

## hammer
A **hammer** is a tool for banging in nails.

## hamster
A **hamster** is a small, furry animal. **Hamsters** keep food in their cheeks.

## hand
We have a **hand** at the end of each arm. Our **hands** are for holding and touching things.

## handkerchief
We use a **handkerchief** to wipe our nose when we have a cold.

## harp
We pluck the strings on a **harp** to make music.

## hat
We wear a **hat** on our heads. This is a man's **hat**.

## hay
Farmers store dried grass, called **hay**, for feeding cows and sheep.

## head
Our **head** is on our shoulders. The face is the front of the head.

## hedge
A **hedge** is a row of bushes which makes a fence round a field or garden.

## heel

The **heel** is the back part of the foot.

## helicopter

A **helicopter** is an aircraft without wings.
**Helicopters** can fly straight up into the air.

## helmet

A **helmet** is a strong cover for the head. We wear a **helmet** to keep our head safe.

## hen

A female bird is called a **hen**. We can eat the eggs of farmyard **hens**.

## hill

A **hill** is higher than the land around it. **Hills** are not as high as mountains.

### hook
We can hang a coat on a **hook**.

### horn
**Horns** are the hard, pointed bits on the heads of deer. A rhino has a **horn** on its nose.

### horse
A **horse** is an animal which is used for riding, or for pulling carts.

### hospital
When we are very sick, we have to go to **hospital**.

## Ii

### iceberg
A very large block of ice which floats in the sea is an **iceberg**.

### ice cream
**Ice cream** is cold and sweet. Eating **ice cream** is great.

### icicles
**Icicles** are pointed spikes of frozen water.

### icing
**Icing** is the sweet topping put on birthday cakes.

## igloo

Eskimos live in houses called **igloos**. An **igloo** is made from frozen snow.

## insects

**Insects** are small animals with six legs. Some **insects** are small, some are big.

## iron

We can press clothes with an **iron**.

## island

An **island** is a piece of land with water all round it.

# Jj

## jack-in-the-box

When you open the lid of a **jack-in-the-box**, a funny toy jumps out.

## jar

We can keep sweets in a **jar**.

## jeans

**Jeans** are trousers made from strong, blue cloth.

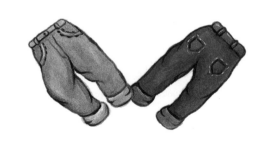

## jelly

**Jelly** is a cold, clear, sweet pudding.

## jellyfish

A **jellyfish** lives in the sea.
**Jellyfish** look as if they are
made of jelly.

## jigsaw

We have to fit together the
pieces of a **jigsaw** puzzle.

## juggler

A **juggler** throws and
catches lots of things all at
once. He **juggles** things in
the air.

## jumper

A knitted pullover with long
sleeves is a **jumper**.

# Kk

## kangaroo
A **kangaroo** is an Australian animal. Baby **kangaroos** are carried in their mother's pouch.

## key
You open a lock with a **key**.

## king
A **king** is the head of a country.

## kiss
The girl is giving the baby a **kiss**.

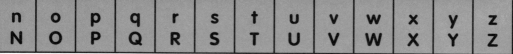

## kite

The boy is flying his **kite**.
He must hold on to the string
of his **kite**.

## kitten

A **kitten** is a young cat.

## knee

Your leg bends in the
middle at the **knee**.

## knife

We cut things with a **knife**.

# Ll

## ladder
You climb a **ladder** to get up to high things.

## ladybird
A **ladybird** is a red or yellow insect with spots on its back.

## lake
A **lake** is a lot of water with land all round it.

46

## lamb
A **lamb** is a young sheep.

## lamp
A **lamp** gives us light. When it gets dark, we switch on the lamp.

## leaf
A **leaf** will grow on a tree or a plant.

## leap-frog
It is fun to play **leap-frog**. In **leap-frog**, you leap over your friends' backs.

## leg

We have two **legs**. The boy is waving one **leg** in the air.

## lemon

A **lemon** is a yellow fruit with a bitter taste.

## leopard

A **leopard** is a large, wild animal with a spotted coat.

## letter

When we write a **letter**, we are sending a message to someone.

## library

A **library** is a room or a building where books are kept.

| n | o | p | q | r | s | t | u | v | w | x | y | z |
|---|---|---|---|---|---|---|---|---|---|---|---|---|
| N | O | P | Q | R | S | T | U | V | W | X | Y | Z |

## lighthouse

A **lighthouse** is a tall building with a light on top to warn ships of danger.

## lightning

**Lightning** is the flash that we see in the sky during a thunderstorm.

## lion

A **lion** is a fierce, wild animal. **Lions** are part of the cat family.

## lizard

A **lizard** is an animal with short legs and a long tail.

## lock

The cupboard has a **lock** on it. You need a key to un**lock** the cupboard.

## locomotive

The machine that pulls a train is called a **locomotive**.

## lollipop

A **lollipop** is a sweet on a stick. We lick a **lollipop**.

# Mm

### machine

A **machine** is something that helps us to do work more easily. We clean clothes in a washing-**machine**.

### magic

The man is doing **magic** tricks. It is difficult to understand how a **magic** trick works.

### mask

The boy is wearing a **mask**. His face is covered with a **mask**.

## mat

A **mat** is like a small rug.
We wipe our feet on a
door**mat**.

## medicine

**Medicine** is something we
take to make us better when
we are not well.

## mermaid

In stories, a **mermaid** is a
woman who lives in the sea.
She has a fish s tail instead
of legs.

## milk

**Milk** is a white drink that
comes from cows.
Children drink lots of **milk**.

## mirror

A **mirror** is a piece of glass
that we can see ourselves in.

### mole
A **mole** is a furry animal that lives underground.

### moneybox
We keep our savings in a **moneybox**. Often a **moneybox** is a fat pig.

### monkey
A **monkey** is a wild, furry animal. **Monkeys** are very good at climbing.

### mountain
A hill that is very high is called a **mountain**.

## mouse

A **mouse** is a tiny animal with a long tail. **Mice** have sharp teeth.

## mouth

A **mouth** is the opening in our face. We talk and eat with our **mouths**.

## mushroom

A **mushroom** is a small plant that grows in woods and fields. **Mushrooms** are shaped like little umbrellas.

## music

**Music** is the nice sound you make when you sing. Guitar **music** also sounds good.

# Nn

### neck

The **neck** is the part of the body that joins the head to the shoulders. Giraffes have very long **necks**.

### necklace

Some people wear a decoration round their neck called a **necklace**.

### needle

We use a **needle** for sewing.

### nest

Birds, and some other animals, make a home called a **nest**.

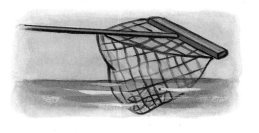

### net
Sometimes a **net** is used for catching fish.

### newt
A **newt** is like a lizard that lives partly in water.

### nose
We breathe and smell through our **nose**.

### nurse
A **nurse** looks after us when we are sick.

### nuts
When we have taken off the hard shells, we can eat **nuts**.

# O o

### oar

An **oar** is a long piece of wood with one flat end. We use **oars** to move a rowing boat.

### ocean

An **ocean** is a very large sea. One **ocean** is the Atlantic **Ocean**.

### octopus

An **octopus** lives in the sea. It has eight long legs with suckers on them.

### onion

**Onions** are good to eat. We cry when we cut an **onion**.

## orange
**Orange** is a colour.
The boy's jumper is **orange**.

## orange
An **orange** is a kind of fruit.
**Oranges** are sweet and
good to eat.

## orchard
A field full of fruit trees is
called an **orchard**.

## orchestra
A lot of people making
music together is called an
**orchestra**.

**ostrich**
The **ostrich** is the largest bird in the world.
An **ostrich** cannot fly.

**otter**
An **otter** is a brown, furry animal. **Otters** can swim well and they eat fish.

**oven**
We cook lots of things like cakes and biscuits in an **oven**.

**overalls**
We wear **overalls** when working, to keep our clothes clean.

**owl**
An **owl** is a bird with a big head and eyes. **Owls** can see well in the dark.

# P p

## pail
Jack and Jill carried a **pail** of water. Another name for a **pail** is a bucket.

## paint
We put **paint** on things to make them bright and pretty. **Paint** comes in cans.

## pancake
A **pancake** is flat and round, and good to eat.

## panda
A **panda** is a big, black and white bear.

60

## parade

It is fun to watch a circus **parade**.

## park

A **park** is a place with grass and trees, where anyone can play.

## parrot

A **parrot** is a colourful bird. **Parrots** can learn to say some words.

## party

At a **party**, we have lots of fun together. Usually we have a party on our birthday.

## paw

A **paw** is an animal's foot with claws. Dogs and cats have **paws**.

## peacock

A **peacock** is a bird with a tail of colourful feathers.

## pen

We can write and draw with a **pen**.

## pets

**Pets** are animals that we keep as special friends.
A **pet** can be a dog, a cat, a rabbit, a canary or a goldfish.

## piano

We can make music with a **piano**.

## picnic

When we eat outdoors, we are having a **picnic**.

## pie

A **pie** is filled with fruit or meat and cooked in the oven.

## pig

A **pig** is a pink animal with a curly tail. We keep **pigs** on farms.

## pigeon

A **pigeon** is a plump bird with short legs. **Pigeons** can find their way home from far away.

## pilot

A pilot is the person who flies an aircraft.

## pink

**Pink** is a colour.
The ballet shoes are **pink**.

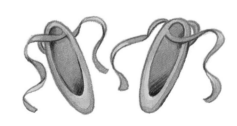

## pirate
A **pirate** is someone who robs from ships.

## pocket
A pocket is like a little bag in our clothes. We can keep lots of things in our **pockets**.

## polar bear
A **polar bear** is a wild animal that lives in very cold places.

## pond
A **pond** is a small patch of water. Sometimes we have a **pond** in the garden.

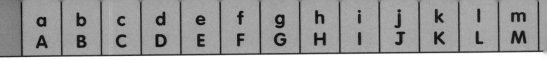

| a | b | c | d | e | f | g | h | i | j | k | l | m |
|---|---|---|---|---|---|---|---|---|---|---|---|---|
| A | B | C | D | E | F | G | H | I | J | K | L | M |

## pony
A **pony** is like a little horse.

## puppet
We play with a **puppet** by moving its strings. There are also **puppets** like gloves.

## puppy
A **puppy** is a young dog.

## purple
**Purple** is a colour.
The flowers are **purple**.

## purse
We put money in a **purse** to keep it safe.

| n | o | p | q | r | s | t | u | v | w | x | y | z |
|---|---|---|---|---|---|---|---|---|---|---|---|---|
| N | O | P | Q | R | S | T | U | V | W | X | Y | Z |

# Q q

**quack**
Ducks **quack**. A **quack** is the sound they make.

**queen**
A **queen** is the head of a country. The wife of a king is also a **queen**.

**quilt**
A **quilt** is the warm, padded cover on our bed.

**quiver**
We carry arrows in a **quiver**.

# Rr

### rabbit

A **rabbit** is a small, furry animal, with very long ears. A **rabbit** is sometimes called a bunny.

### race

We have a **race** to see who is the fastest at something. The children are in a swimming **race**.

### raft

A **raft** is a flat boat made out of wood.

## railway

A **railway** is the rail track that trains and trams run on.

## rain

**Rain** falls on us from the clouds. We get wet when it is **raining**.

## rainbow

When the sun shines after it has rained, we sometimes see a **rainbow** in the sky.

## rattle

A baby will play with a **rattle**. A **rattle** makes a rattling noise.

## red

**Red** is a colour.
The bus is **red**.

## reindeer

A **reindeer** is an animal with very large horns.

## ring

Sometimes we wear a **ring** on our finger. A **ring** is a circle.

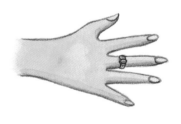

## river

A **river** is a large stream of moving water. Some **rivers** move slowly, some move fast.

## robot

This toy **robot** is a machine in the shape of a person.

### rocket
A **rocket** shoots up into the air. It is fun to see **rockets** when they are fireworks.

### rocking horse
When we are little, we can play on a **rocking horse**.

### roller skates
We can move fast when we play on **roller skates**.

### root
A **root** is the part of a tree or a plant under the ground.

### runway
Aircraft land and take off from a **runway**. A **runway** is a road for aircraft.

# S s

### saddle
You sit in a **saddle** when you ride a horse.

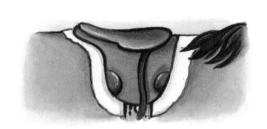

### sail
The wind blows into the **sail** and moves the boat along.

### salad
A **salad** is a mixture of vegetables or fruit. **Salads** are cold.

### sandcastle
It is fun to build a **sandcastle** on the beach.

## Santa Claus

**Santa Claus** brings us presents at Christmas.

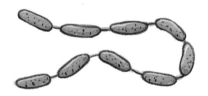

### sausages

Here is a string of **sausages**. Most children enjoy eating **sausages**.

### saw

A **saw** has a sharp, jagged edge. We cut things with a **saw**.

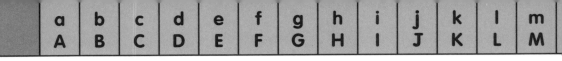

| a | b | c | d | e | f | g | h | i | j | k | l | m |
|---|---|---|---|---|---|---|---|---|---|---|---|---|
| A | B | C | D | E | F | G | H | I | J | K | L | M |

## school

People go to **school** to learn things. Children learn to read and write at **school**.

## scissors

**Scissors** will cut paper and cloth. We say that we have a pair of **scissors**.

## sea

The **sea** is the water that covers most of the earth. **Sea** water is salty.

## seal

A **seal** is an animal with fur and flippers. **Seals** spend most of their time in the sea.

## seashells
We can find lots of **seashells** beside the sea. A little animal used to live in every **seashell**.

## see-saw
The children are playing on the **see-saw**.

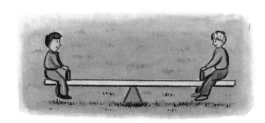

## shadow
A light in front of us makes a **shadow** behind us.
A **shadow** is the dark shape we make in the light.

## shark
A **shark** lives in the sea.
Some **sharks** eat people!

## sheep
We keep **sheep** on farms.
Wool is made from a **sheep's** coat.

## ship

We travel across the sea in a **ship**.
Some **ships** are very big.

## shop

We can buy things in a **shop**.

## shower

A **shower** sprays us with water so that we can wash ourselves.

## signpost

A **signpost** points the way to somewhere.

## singer

Someone who makes music with their voice is a **singer**.

## skateboard

A **skateboard** is a board with wheels on it. You can move about and do tricks on a **skateboard**.

## skeleton

Our **skeleton** is made up of all the bones in our body.

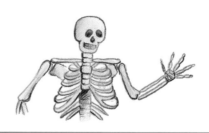

## sleep

We go to bed to **sleep**. When we are tired, we need to have a **sleep**.

## sleigh

We travel over the snow in a **sleigh**. Santa uses a **sleigh** to deliver presents.

## smoke

**Smoke** is the dark cloud that we see when something is burning.

## snail

A **snail** is a small animal with a shell on its back. **Snails** move very slowly.

## snake

**Snakes** are long, thin animals without legs. A **snake** slides along the ground.

## snow

When it is cold, flakes of frozen water called **snow** fall from the sky.

## spider

A **spider** is a small animal with eight legs.
**Spiders** make a web to catch their food.

## squirrel

A **squirrel** is a red or grey animal with a bushy tail.
**Squirrels** live in trees.

## stars

We see lots of tiny lights in the sky at night. They are the **stars**.

## starfish

A **starfish** is a star-shaped fish. You will sometimes find one at the edge of the sea.

## steeple

A **steeple** is the high, pointed top of a church.

## storm

It is a **storm** when there are strong winds and heavy rain.

## street

A road with houses or shops along it is a **street**.

## submarine

A **submarine** is a boat that can go under the water.

## sunflower

A **sunflower** is a large, golden flower. A **sunflower** always faces the sun.

## supermarket

A very big shop is called a **supermarket**.

## swan

A **swan** is a big, white bird with a very long neck.

# T t

## tail

A **tail** is the end of something.
Most animals have **tails**.

## tambourine

Sometimes we make music with a **tambourine**.

## tangle

The dogs' leads are in a **tangle**. They are all knotted together.

## taxi

A **taxi** is a car that will take us places for money.
**Taxi** is short for **taxi**cab.

## teacher

The **teacher** teaches us things at school. We learn things from a **teacher**.

## Teddy bear

A **Teddy bear** is soft and warm.

## telephone

We talk on the **telephone** to someone far away.
A **telephone** is a **phone**.

## television

**Television** shows us pictures in our homes from far away.

### tent
When we are camping, we sleep in a **tent**.

### theatre
We go to the **theatre** to see actors, and to hear music.

### thermometer
When we are not well, a **thermometer** measures how hot we are.

### thumb
On each hand, we have a **thumb** and four other fingers.

### tiger
A **tiger** is a big, wild animal with a striped coat.

### toes
We have five **toes** on the end of each foot.

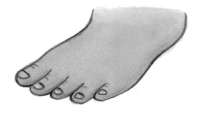

### tomato
A **tomato** is a soft red fruit. We eat **tomatoes** raw or cooked.

### tools
**Tools** help us to do work. A screwdriver is a **tool**.

### tooth
A **tooth** is one of the hard white bones in our mouth. We bite things with our **teeth**.

### tortoise
A **tortoise** is a slow-moving animal with a hard shell on its back.

### tower
The walls of a castle have **towers** at each corner. A **tower** is a tall, narrow building.

### toys
**Toy** boats, **toy** ducks, and **toy** drums are all **toys**.

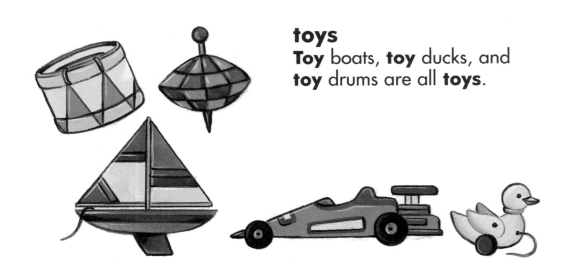

### tractor
A **tractor** can pull heavy things over muddy ground.

## train

A **train** is pulled by a locomotive. Sometimes there are lots of wagons in a **train**.

## tree

A **tree** is a very big plant. **Trees** have branches and leaves.

## truck

Lots of things are carried by road in a **truck**.

## trumpet

We can make music by blowing a **trumpet**.

## tunnel

A **tunnel** is a passage under the ground.

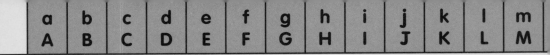
# Uu

### umbrella
An **umbrella** will keep us dry when it rains.

### unicorn
In fairy tales, a **unicorn** is a magic animal, like a horse with one horn on its head.

### uniform
A **uniform** is a set of special clothes that some people wear. A nurse wears a **uniform**.

# Vv

## vacuum cleaner
A **vacuum cleaner** is a machine that sucks up dirt.

## valley
A **valley** is the low piece of land between hills. Often a river goes through a **valley**.

## van
A small truck for delivering things is called a **van**.

## vase
We put flowers in a **vase**.

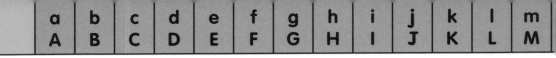

## vegetables

**Vegetables** are plants that we grow for food. We eat lots of **vegetables**. They are good for us.

## violin

We can make music on a **violin** by rubbing a stick called a bow against the **violin** strings.

## voice

When we sing we are using our **voice**. We also use our **voice** to speak.

# W w

### wagon
A **wagon** is a cart for carrying heavy loads. Sometimes a **wagon** is pulled by horses.

### waist
Our **waist** is in the middle of our body. Our body bends at the **waist**.

### walrus
A **walrus** is a big sea animal with long tusks.

### watch
A **watch** is like a small clock that we wear on our arm.

## waterfall

A stream of water falling over a cliff is called a **waterfall**.

## well

A **well** is a deep hole in the ground with water in it.

## whale

A **whale** is a big animal that lives in the sea.

## wheelbarrow

We use a **wheelbarrow** in the garden.
A **wheelbarrow** has two handles and one wheel.

## wigwam

A **wigwam** is a kind of tent that some American Indians used to live in.

## windmill

The wind blows round the sails of a **windmill**. **Windmills** are machines that can lift water.

## wing

The **wing** is the part of a bird that it uses to fly. Birds have two **wings**.

## woodpecker

A **woodpecker** is a bird that pecks wood. You can often hear a **woodpecker** tapping on a tree.

## worm

A **worm** is like a little snake that lives in the earth.

## wrist

Our **wrist** joins our hand to our arm. We have two **wrists**.

# Xx

## X-rays

A picture of the inside of our body is called an **x-ray**.

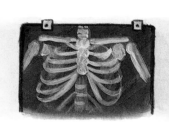

## xylophone

We play a **xylophone** to make music.

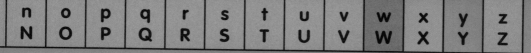

| n | o | p | q | r | s | t | u | v | w | x | y | z |
|---|---|---|---|---|---|---|---|---|---|---|---|---|
| N | O | P | Q | R | S | T | U | V | W | X | Y | Z |

# Yy

## yacht
A boat with large sails is called a **yacht**.

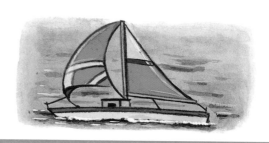

## yawn
We **yawn** when we are tired. When we **yawn** we open our mouth wide.

## yellow
**Yellow** is a colour. The little bird is **yellow**.

## yo-yo
A **yo-yo** is a toy. We spin a **yo-yo** up and down.

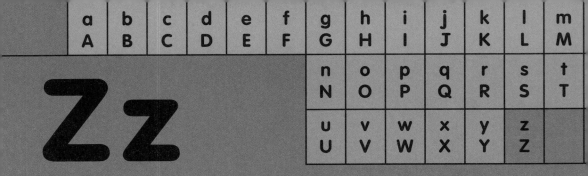

| a | b | c | d | e | f | g | h | i | j | k | l | m |
|---|---|---|---|---|---|---|---|---|---|---|---|---|
| A | B | C | D | E | F | G | H | I | J | K | L | M |
| | | | | | | n | o | p | q | r | s | t |
| | | | | | | N | O | P | Q | R | S | T |
| | | | | | | u | v | w | x | y | z | |
| | | | | | | U | V | W | X | Y | Z | |

# Zz

### zebra
A **zebra** is a wild animal like a striped horse.

### zip
A **zip** fastens parts of our clothes together. Sometimes we have a **zip** at the front of our jacket.

clock

butterfly

parrot

# My First 1000 WORDS

rocket

tractor

flower

father

mother

brother

sister

# contents

grandmother
(father's mother)

father, dad,
husband

mother, mum,
wife

grandfather
(father's father)

son, brother

daughter,
sister

cousin
(aunt's daughter)

cousin
(uncle's son)

aunt (mother's sister)

uncle
(mother's brother)

# our bodies

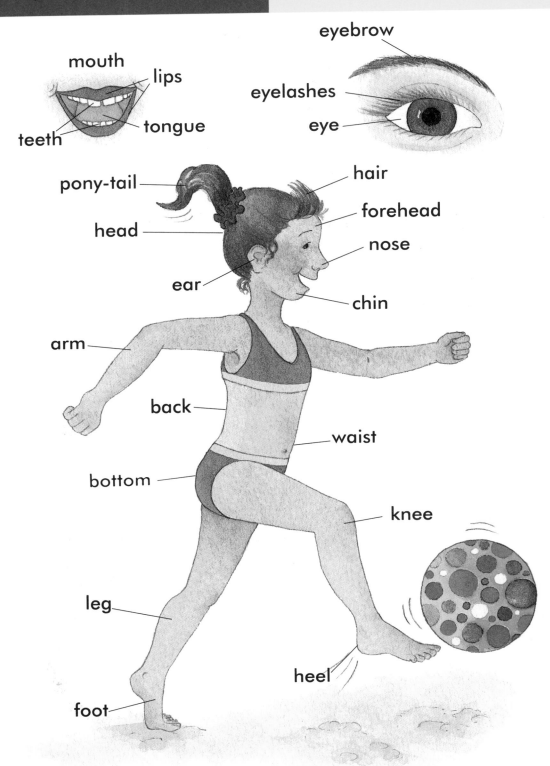

mouth

lips

tongue

teeth

eyebrow

eyelashes

eye

pony-tail

hair

head

forehead

nose

ear

chin

arm

back

waist

bottom

knee

leg

heel

foot

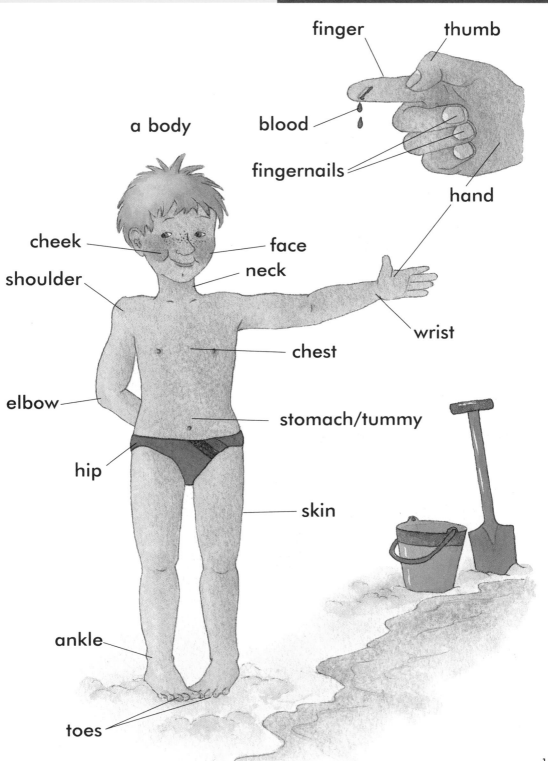

finger

thumb

blood

fingernails

hand

a body

cheek

face

neck

shoulder

wrist

chest

elbow

stomach/tummy

hip

skin

ankle

toes

# more people words

bald

man

people

parents

moustache

beard

boy

bride

hear

taste

twins

bridegroom

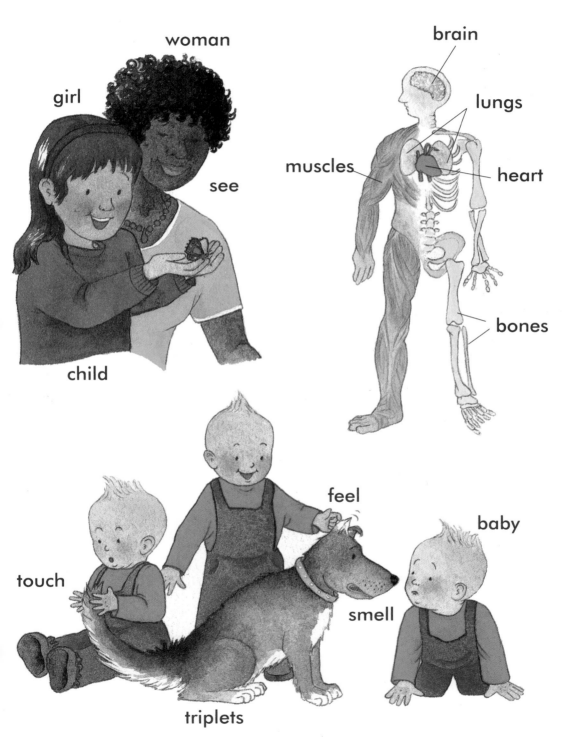

woman

girl

see

brain

lungs

muscles

heart

child

bones

feel

baby

touch

smell

triplets

# clothes

 dress

 jumper

 hat

knickers

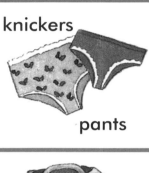 pants

 dressing gown

 trousers

 anorak

socks

blouse

 skirt

pyjamas

petticoat

leggings

coat

cap

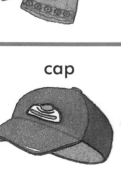

shorts

raincoat

T-shirt

tights

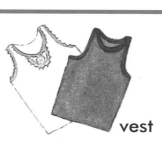 vest

jacket

 scarf

nightdress 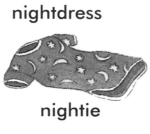 nightie

jeans

underpants

 cardigan

 rainhat

 sweater

shirt

track suit

# more things to wear

laces

slippers

earrings

tie

buttonhole

handkerchief/
hankie

braces

button

suit

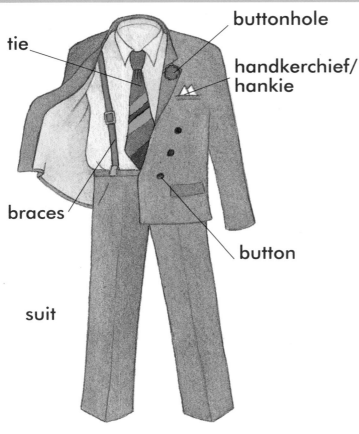

necklace

rubber boots

glasses

shoes

mittens

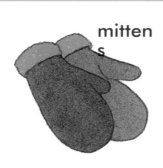

apron

# more things to wear

overalls

boots

gloves

ring

trainers

belt

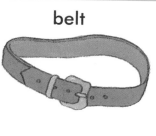

buckle

tiara

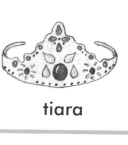

swimsuit

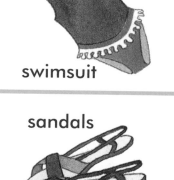

ribbon

hairband

brooch

bracelet

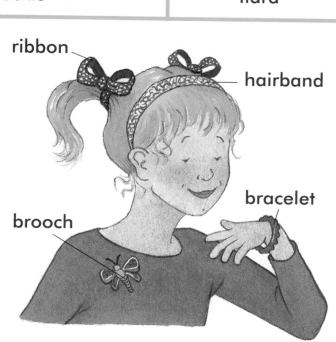

sandals

trunks

# the bedroom

bedside table

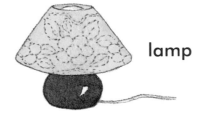
lamp

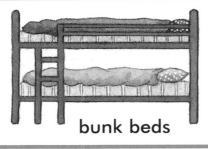
bunk beds

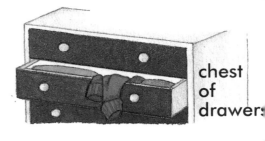
chest of drawers

eiderdown

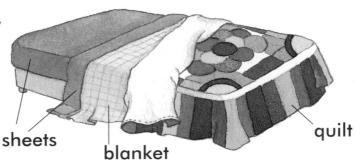
sheets

blanket

quilt

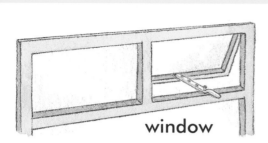
window

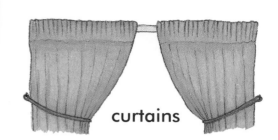
curtains

alarm clock

wardrobe

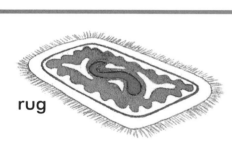
rug

bed
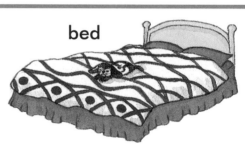

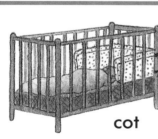
cot

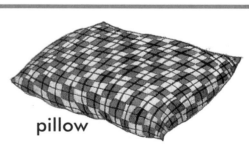
pillow

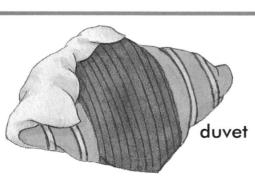
duvet

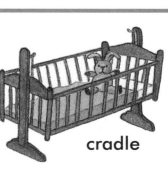
cradle

# the bathroom

plug

plug-hole

sponge

bath

bubbles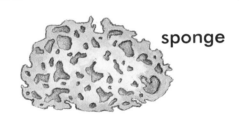

toilet

toilet paper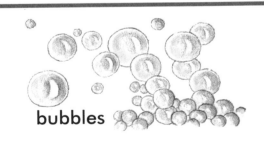

wash-basin

towel

shower-curtain

bidet

towel-rail

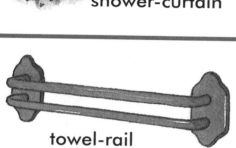

soap

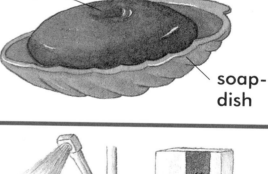

soap-dish

toothpaste

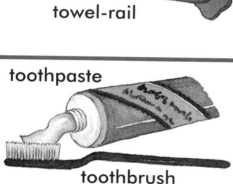

toothbrush

shower

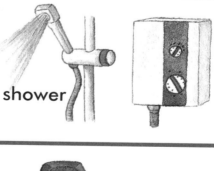

tap

potty

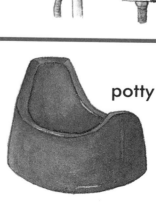

# the kitchen

 food-mixer

 kettle

coffee pot

 cupboard

cooker

 oven

draining board

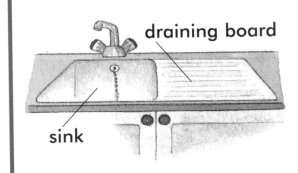 sink

teapot

vacuum cleaner

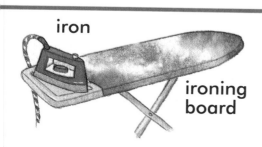
iron

ironing board

washing machine

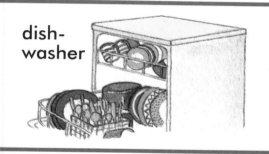
dish-washer

switch

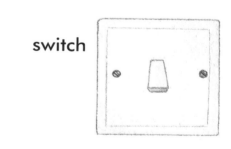

refrigerator/fridge

socket

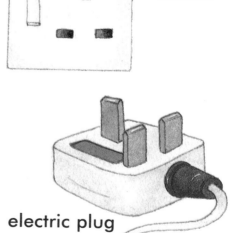

electric plug

freezer

# the living-room

books

book-ends

remote control

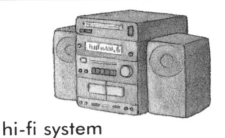

hi-fi system

vase of flowers

gas fire

door-handle

door

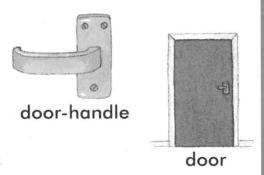

screen

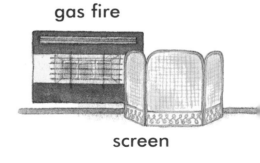

painting

magazine rack

newspapers

magazines

comics

telephone/phone

video cassette

video recorder

television set/TV

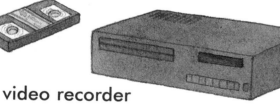
cushions

photographs

mantlepiece

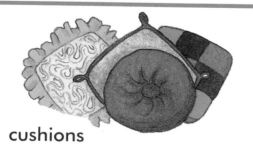

fireplace

radio

# the dining-room

table-cloth

plates

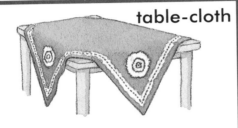

cup

saucer

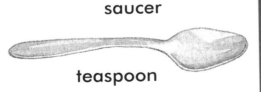

teaspoon

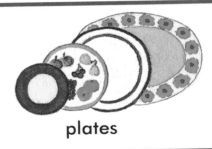

oil

vinegar

mirror

# the dining-room

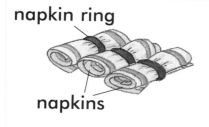

napkin ring

napkins

fork

spoon

table-mat

knife

candles

candlestick

salt

pepper

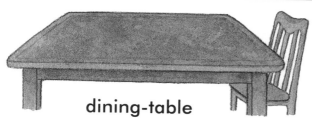

dining-table

chairs

eggcups

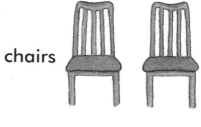

jug

tumbler

fruit bowl

bottle

wine-glasses

# the playroom

**toys**

rocking horse

soft toys

playpen

train set

building blocks

toy soldiers

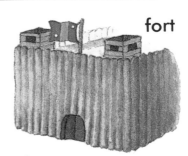

fort

118

# the playroom

toy duck

toy boats

spinning top

teddy bear

toy cars

counting frame

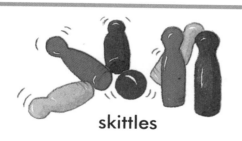

skittles

doll's house

playhouse

doll's pram

# things in the house

hatstand

settee/sofa

armchair

bench

beanbag

footstool

rug

stool

high-chair

rocking-chair

# things in the house

bookcase

table
lamp

sideboard

grandfather
clock

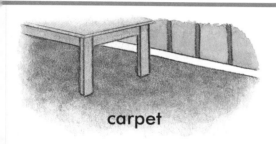
carpet

coffee table

candelabra

dressing-table

breakfast bar

# the garden

greenhouse

shed

hedge

watering-can

compost heap

vegetable plot

rake

bushes

wheelbarrow

garden fork

spade

flower-bed

sprinkler

hoe

flowers

chimney

TV aerial

roof

bonfire

drain-pipe

gutter

porch

ladder

front door

window box

barrel

roof tiles

grass lawn

path

lawnmower

hosepipe

123

# in the workshop

ramp

tyres

car jack

tyre lever

foot-pump

car battery

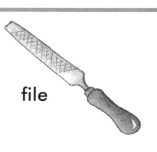

paint-brushes

saw

sandpaper

paint pots

nuts and bolts

file

spanners

pickaxe

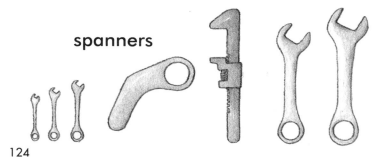

oilcan

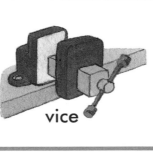 vice

axe

drill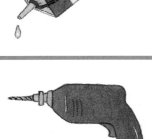

penknife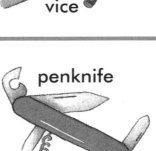

wooden plank

screwdriver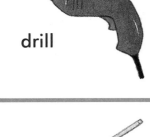

screws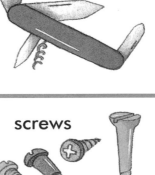

bucket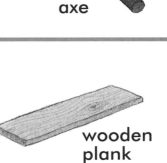

toolbox

plane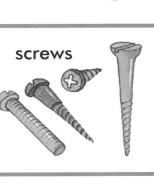

hammer

tape-measure

pliers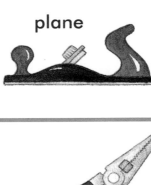

nails

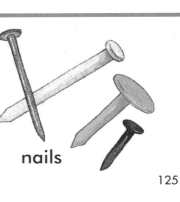

# friendly pets

mouse

toad

hamster

rat

frog

guinea-pig

gerbil

rabbit

cat

basket

tortoise

kitten

fishbowl

kennel

newt

goldfish

terrapin

dog

puppy

hedgehog

silkworm

stick-insect

pigeon

budgerigar

canary

lizard

mynah bird

lovebirds

birdcage

horse

parrot

foal

Shetland
pony

127

# out in the street

phone booth

bus stop

parking meter

corner

crossing

roundabout

road sign

street-light

bollard

traffic lights

kerb

pavement

road works

road

bicycle

 bus

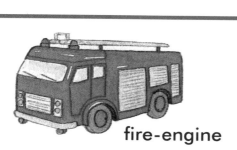 fire-engine

taxi

car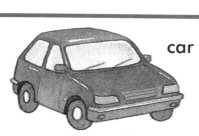

road-roller

lorry

motor-cycle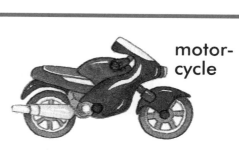

police car

van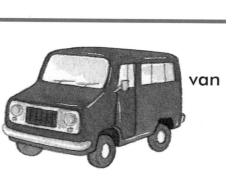

# in town

church

restaurant

market

houses

hotel

skyscraper

post office

shop

car park

theatre

bank

factory

pub

park

school

supermarket

library

cinema

police station

office block

131

# in the supermarket

breakfast cereal

sausages

meat

fruit juice

chicken

eggs

ham

fish

jam

chocolate bars

turnstile

cans of beans

# in the supermarket

cheese

butter

milk

till

credit card

money

receipt

check-out desk

trolley

purse

handbag

shopping bag

# all kinds of fruit

orange

grapes

banana

cherries

lemon

pineapple

apple

redcurrants
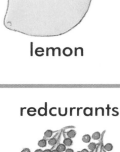

plums

gooseberries

grapefruit

pear

blackberries

melon

strawberries

# lots of vegetables

cabbage

tomatoes

cucumber

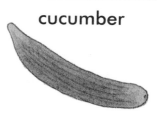

potatoes

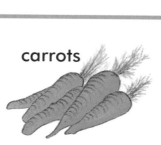
pumpkin

peas

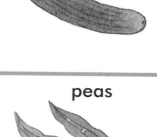

corn on the cob

carrots

onions

leeks

green beans

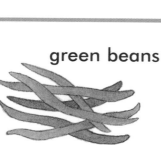

cauliflower

lettuce

mushrooms

sprouts

# more things to eat and drink

cake

hot dog

rice

honey

jelly

coconut

toast

milk shake

pack of spaghetti

doughnuts

lollipop

jellybabies

fish fingers

pancakes

bottle of cola

ice cream

buns

sausage roll

nuts

bag of sugar

chips

tomato sauce

bar of chocolate

salad

apple pie

can of soup

biscuits

sandwich

loaf of bread

pizza

# fun in the park

kite

railings

litter-bin

notice board

bandstand

picnic

scooter

park keeper

sand-pit

fountain

pond

toy yacht

# fun in the park

swings

climbing frame

slide

see-saw

roundabout

skipping rope

path

helmet

drinking fountain

roller skates

pads

lead

collar

dog muzzle

# people at work

actor

secretary

gardener

musician

decorator

shop-keeper

astronaut

diver

cook

singer

dancer

hairdresser

artist

baker

postman

farmer

carpenter

butcher

# more people at work

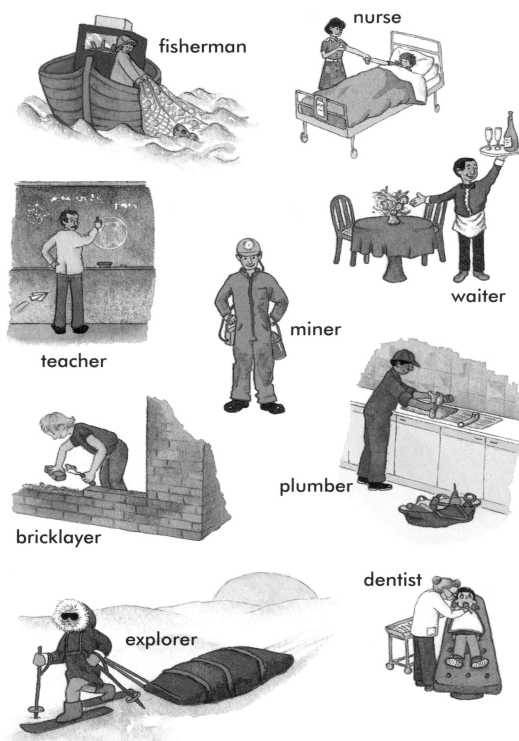

fisherman

nurse

teacher

miner

waiter

bricklayer

plumber

explorer

dentist

clown

judge

porter

TV announcer

fireman

window cleaner

doctor

scientist

electrician

143

# in the office

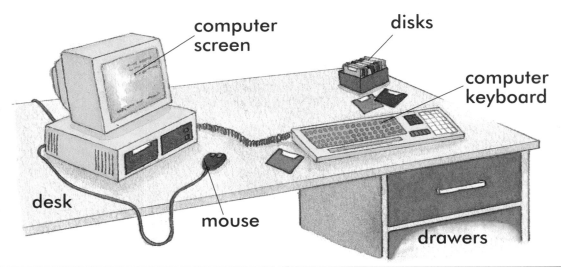

computer screen

disks

computer keyboard

desk

mouse

drawers

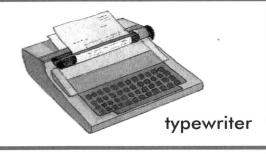

typewriter

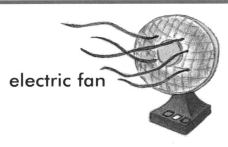

electric fan

swivel chair

fax machine

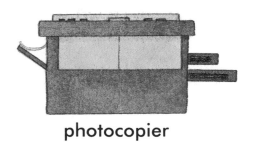

photocopier

writing paper

envelopes

calendar

filing cabinet

pen pencil

pencil sharpener

rubber

ruler
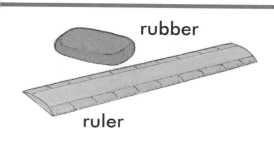

stapler
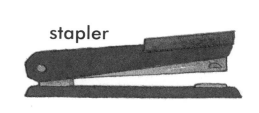

paperweight
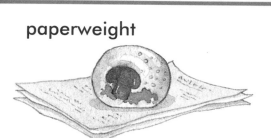

calculator
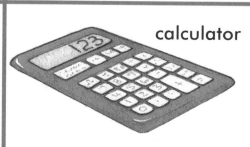

wastepaper bin

coffee machine
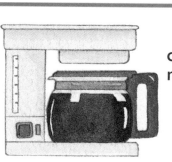

# at the garage

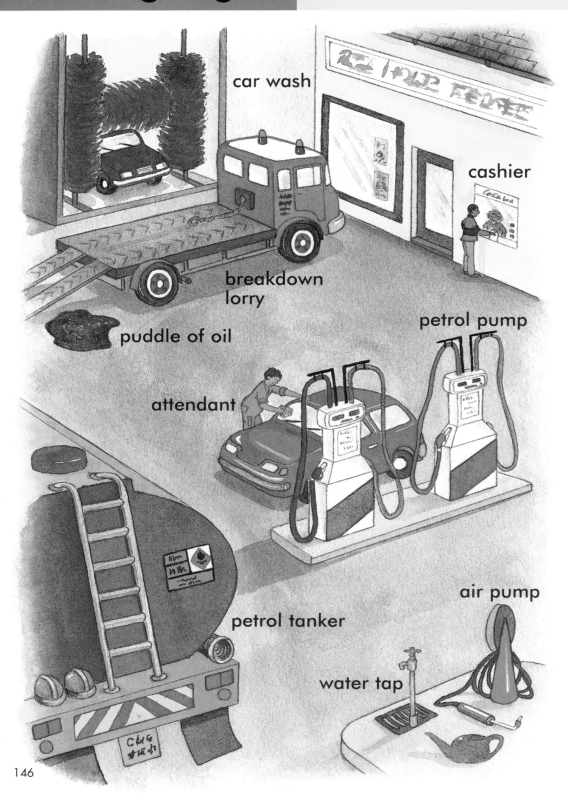

car wash

cashier

breakdown lorry

puddle of oil

petrol pump

attendant

petrol tanker

air pump

water tap

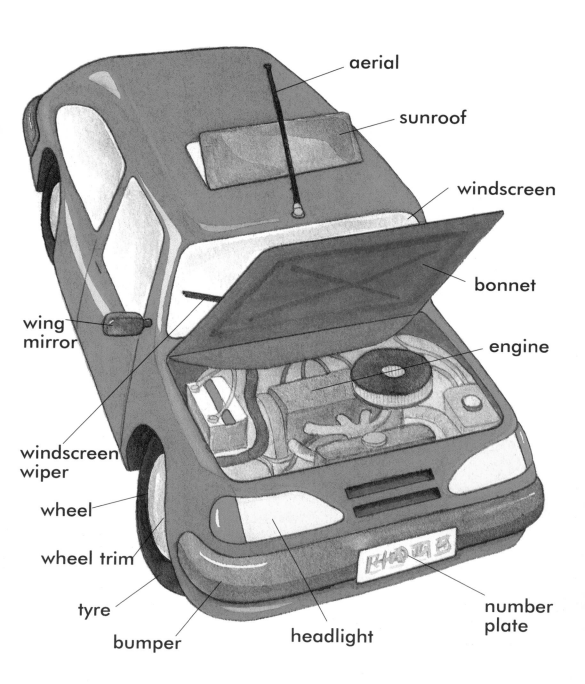

aerial

sunroof

windscreen

bonnet

engine

wing mirror

windscreen wiper

wheel

wheel trim

tyre

bumper

headlight

number plate

# at the doctor

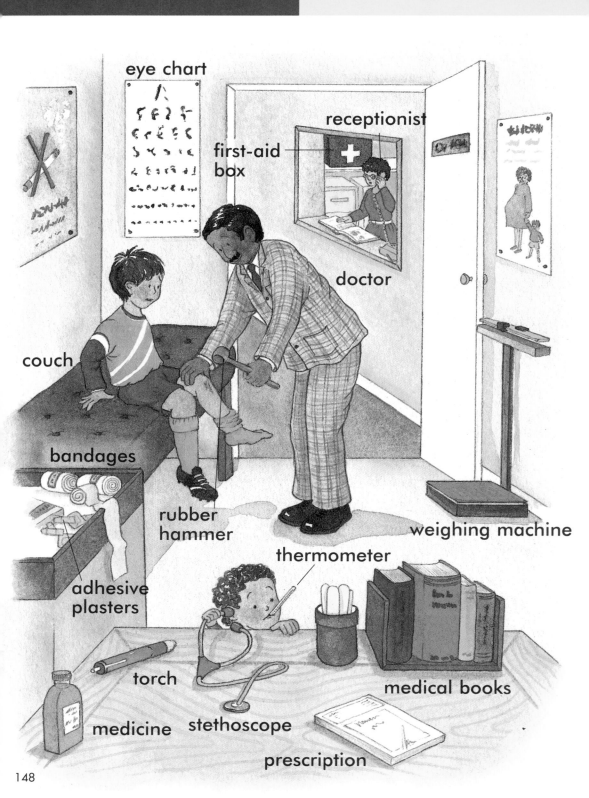

eye chart

first-aid box

receptionist

doctor

couch

bandages

rubber hammer

thermometer

weighing machine

adhesive plasters

torch

medicine

stethoscope

medical books

prescription

big smile

bright light

dentist

fillings

dental nurse

record chart

mask

drill

glass of mouthwash

bib

gown

probe

dentist's mirror

dentist's chair

false teeth

# in hospital

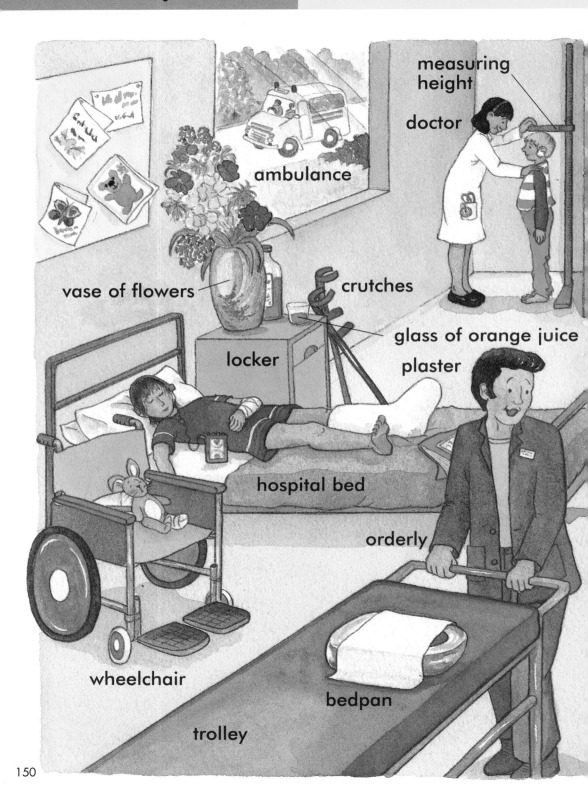

measuring height

doctor

ambulance

vase of flowers

crutches

glass of orange juice

locker

plaster

hospital bed

orderly

wheelchair

bedpan

trolley

lift

X-RAY DEPT.

DO NOT ENTER WHEN RED LIGHT IS ON

x-ray machine

x-ray

curtain

consultant

nurse

chart

syringe

tray

potty

slippers

scissors

# games and pastimes

reading

writing

blindman's buff

dressing-up

singing

sewing

board game

collecting stamps

sleeping

chess

computer game

walking

listening to music

dancing

playing cards

leapfrog

making music

gardening

# sports

canoeing

American football

diving

tennis

showjumping

basketball

skating

rugby

cycling

gymnastics

swimming

baseball

skiing

cricket

table tennis

running

football

horse-riding

# on the farm

sheep    lamb

cow

calf

ducklings    duck

milk
churns

orchard

cockerel

# on the farm

haystack

turkey

goose

goslings

horse

foal

bull

tractor

goat

kid

pig

piglet

hen

chicks

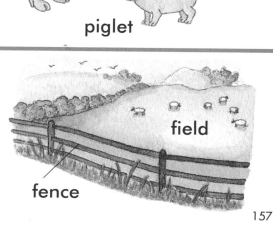
field

fence

157

# at school

lunch-box

pupils

globe

pot of paste

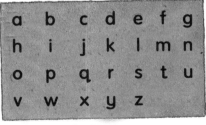

a b c d e f g
h i j k l m n
o p q r s t u
v w x y z

alphabet

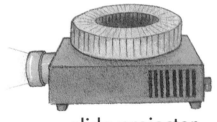
slide projector

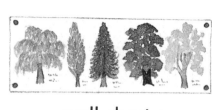

wall chart

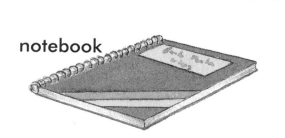

notebook

teacher

blackboard

easel

satchel

duster

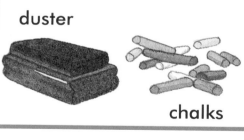

chalks

drawing

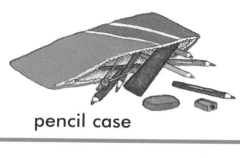

pencil case

modelling clay

writing

# going places: by train

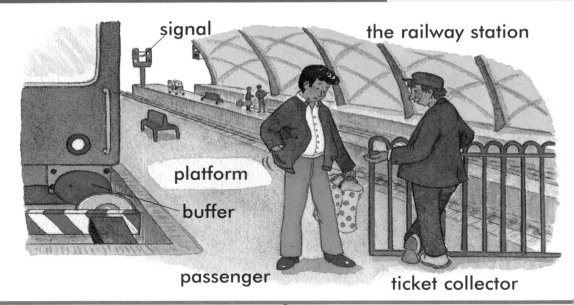

signal

the railway station

platform

buffer

passenger

ticket collector

escalator

diesel engine

level crossing

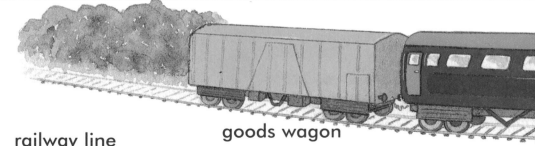

railway line

goods wagon

carriage

# going places: by train

ticket office

buffet car

porter

luggage

tunnel

underground railway

monorail

signal box

smoke

steam engine

161

# going places: by water

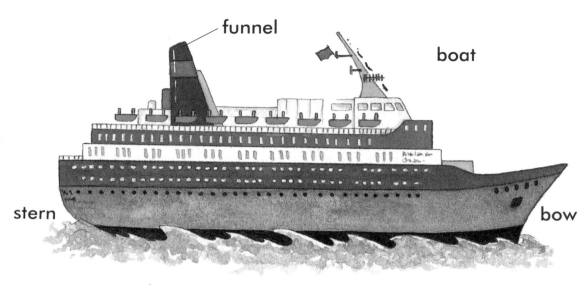

funnel

boat

stern

bow

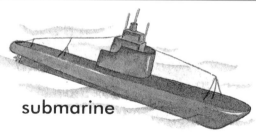

mast

tug-boat

yacht

submarine

anchor

buoy

hydrofoil

# going places: by water

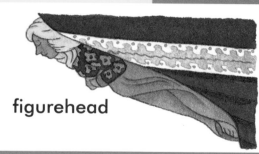
figurehead

rowing boat — oar

barge

hovercraft

paddle-steamer

flag

speedboat
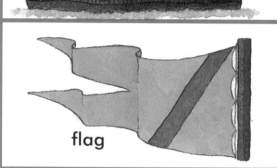

ferry-boat

houseboat

sails

163

# going places: by plane

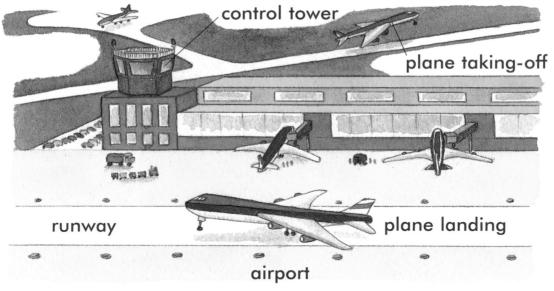

control tower

plane taking-off

runway

plane landing

airport

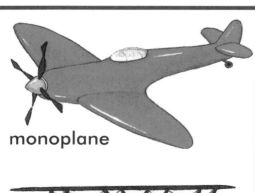

monoplane

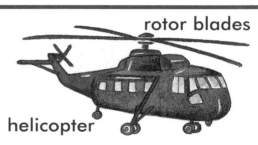

rotor blades

helicopter

biplane

fuel tanker

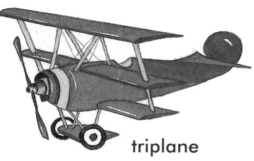

triplane

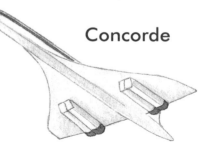

Concorde

# going places: by plane

air hostess

seaplane

passenger jet

propeller

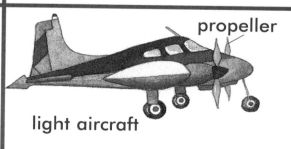

light aircraft

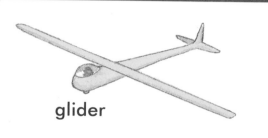

glider

jumbo jet

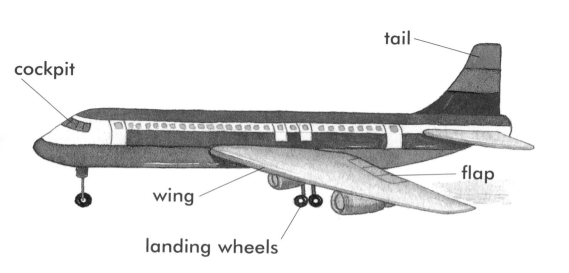

tail

cockpit

flap

wing

landing wheels

# in the country

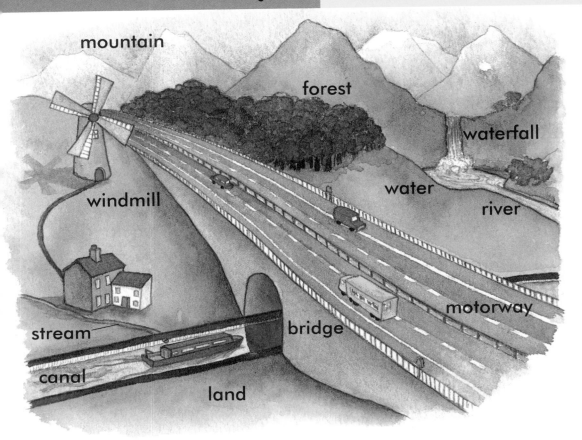

mountain

forest

waterfall

water

river

windmill

motorway

stream

bridge

canal

land

rocks

hiker

map

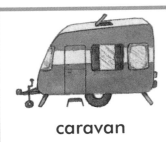

caravan

tent

camper

campfire

sleeping bag

**fishing rod**

**fishing net**

**fisherman**

**trees**

**scarecrow**

**wild flowers**

**stepping stones**

**village**

**town**

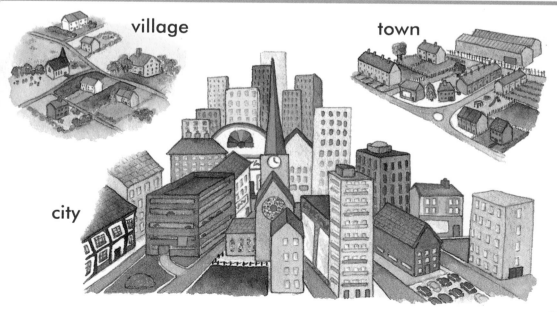

**city**

# builders and buildings

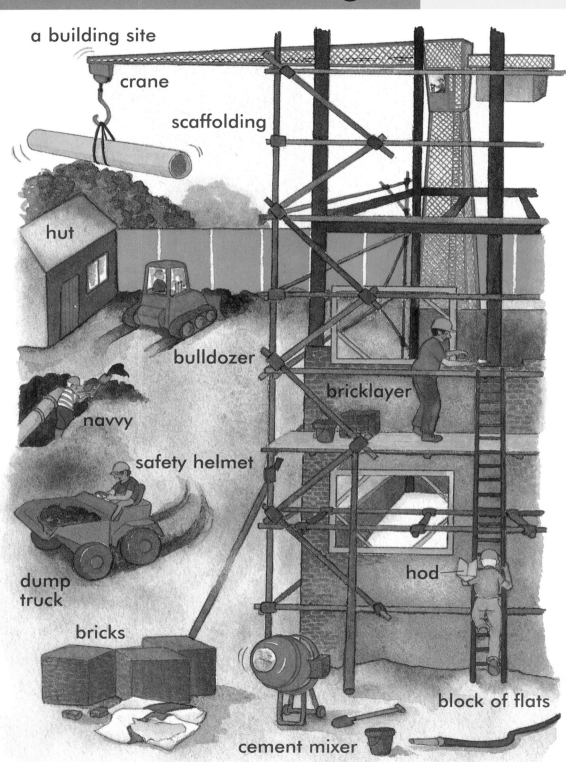

a building site

crane

scaffolding

hut

bulldozer

navvy

safety helmet

dump truck

bricks

bricklayer

hod

cement mixer

block of flats

# builders and buildings

fire station

terraced houses

cottage

mosque

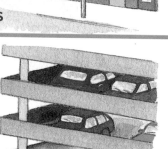
car park

hospital
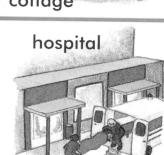

art gallery

hangar

stately home

boathouse

museum

tower

# seasons and weather

winter

spring

lightning

sunshine

summer

autumn

rainbow

rain

storm

hail

ice

snow

170

# tiny animals

cobweb

spider

ladybird

beetle

snail

centipede

earwig

praying mantis

wasp

scorpion

caterpillar

bee

chrysalis

butterfly

beehive

slug

# wild animals

peacock

owl

monkey

ostrich

tiger

lion

giraffe

elephant

gorilla

woodpecker

penguin

stork

swan

porcupine

panda

crocodile

zebra

rhinoceros/rhino

hippopotamus/hippo

whale

# more wild animals

octopus

dolphin

lobster

swordfish

manta ray

moose

shark

camel

polar bear

# more wild animals

platypus

armadillo

kangaroo

seahorse

leopard

koala

sloth

cobra

boa constrictor

seal

walrus

# animal parts

wing

feather

antlers

beak

tail

whiskers

paw

hoof

fin

shell

flipper

pouch

hump

tusk

trunk

# plants

## parts of a flower

petal

bud

leaf

stem

roots

holly

bulb

cactus

wheat growing

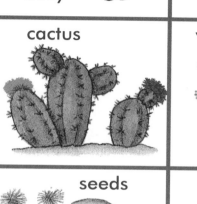

seeds

indoor plant

shoots

rushes

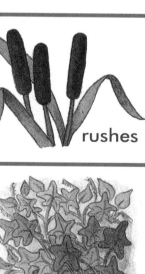

bramble

bush

creeper

twig

branch

trunk

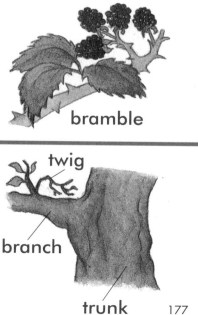

177

# beside the sea

seagulls

boatman

water-skier

donkey

windsurfer

crab

mussels

shellfish

jellyfish

seaweed

pool

starfish

sandcastle

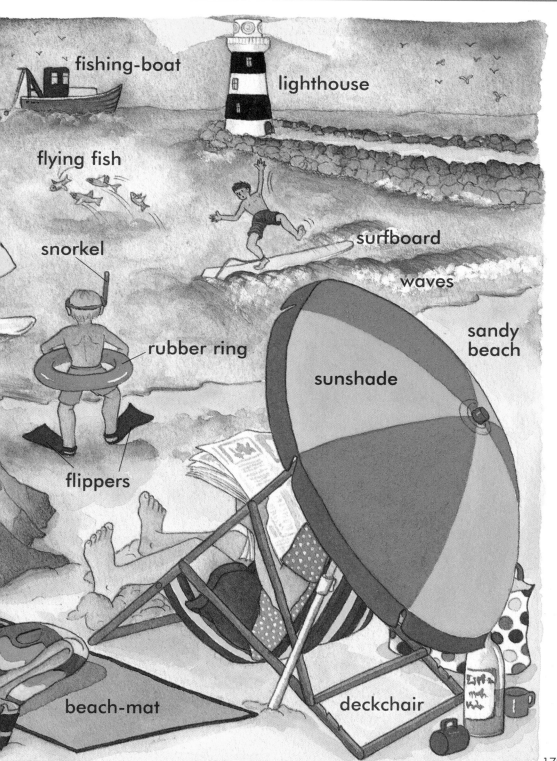

fishing-boat

lighthouse

flying fish

snorkel

surfboard

waves

rubber ring

sunshade

sandy beach

flippers

beach-mat

deckchair

paper chain

balloons

cloak

birthday cards

candles

paper hat

iced cake

sweets

biscuits

sandwiches

crackers

fizzy drinks

chocolates

straws

crumbs

sparklers

magician

party invitation

Please come to my fancy dress party

hostess

guest

presents

ribbon

fancy dress costumes

# opposites

over

under

in

out

up

down

happy

sad

high

low

wet

dry

fast

slow

fat

thin

above

below

big

small

behind

in front

# storybook words

ghost

witch

pirate

dwarf

fairy

dragon

giant

wizard

mermaid

dinosaur

184

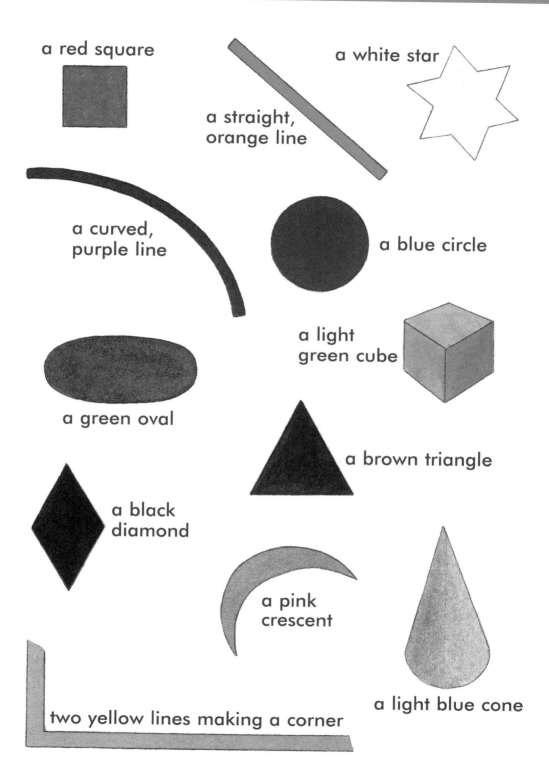

a red square

a straight,
orange line

a white star

a curved,
purple line

a blue circle

a light
green cube

a green oval

a brown triangle

a black
diamond

a pink
crescent

a light blue cone

two yellow lines making a corner

# numbers

1 one girl

2 two boys

3 three ponies

4 four cows

5 five puppies

6 six kittens

7 seven lambs

8 eight pigs

9 nine ducks

10 ten mice

# Words in this Book

ISBN : 0-7097-1384-3
This edition first published 2000 by Brown Watson
The Old Mill, 76 Fleckney Road,
Kibworth Beauchamp,
Leicestershire LE8 0HG, England

Printed in Egypt